Understanding 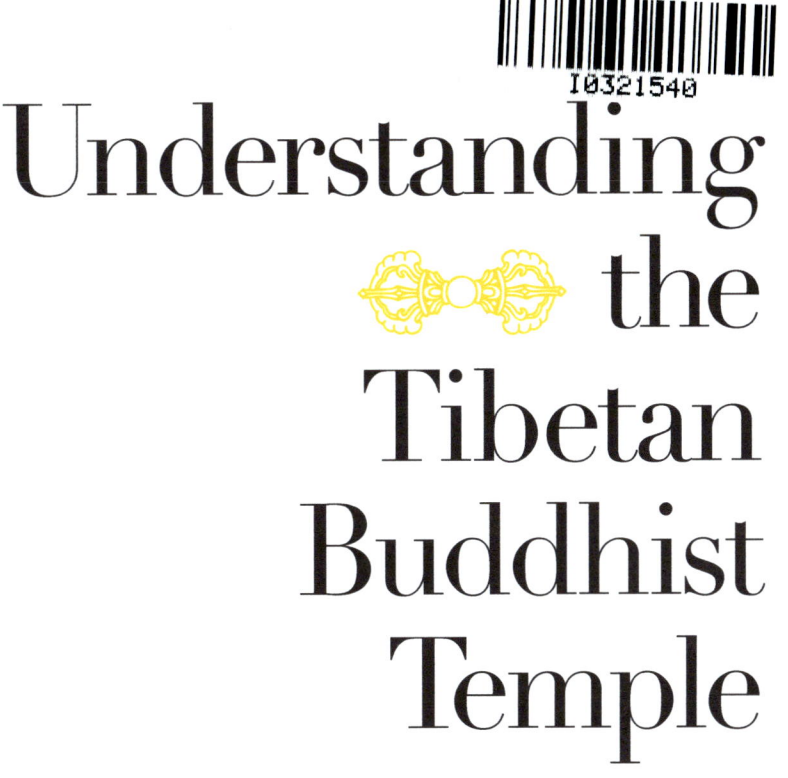 the Tibetan Buddhist Temple

A photographic study of Vajrayana shrine offerings

John Harvey Negru

UNDERSTANDING THE TIBETAN BUDDHIST TEMPLE
A Photographic Study of Vajrayana Shrine Offerings
John Harvey Negru

Text, photographs and design © by John Harvey Negru, 2018
All rights reserved

Published by
The Sumeru Press Inc.
301 Bayrose Drive, Suite 402
Nepean, ON
Canada K2J 5W3

LIBRARY AND ARCHIVES CANADA CATALOGUING IN PUBLICATION

Negru, John, 1951-, author
    Understanding the Tibetan Buddhist temple : a photographic study of Vajrayana shrine offerings / John Harvey Negru.

"This small book is an annotated collection of photographs of statues, shrine offerings, paintings, and other objects at Karma
    Tekchen Zabsal Ling, a Vajrayana Buddhist Temple in Aurora, Ontario. The temple is affiliated with the Thrangu lineage
    and is part of the Karma Kargyu school of Tibetan Buddhism. The photographs were taken over multiple sessions between
    2008 and 2018. KTZL is under the auspices of HH the 17th Karmapa and it is also the home of Lama Tashi Dondup, a
    man of great gentleness and generosity."--Foreword.

ISBN 978-1-896559-07-0 (softcover)

    1. Karma Tekchen Zabsal Ling. 2. Buddhist shrines--Ontario--Aurora.
3. Buddhist shrines--Ontario--Aurora--Pictorial works. 4. Buddhist
temples--Ontario--Aurora. 5. Buddhist temples--Ontario--Aurora--Pictorial
works. 6. Tantric Buddhism--Ontario--Aurora. I. Title.

BQ6379.A972K37 2018   294.3'43509713547   C2018-901354-0

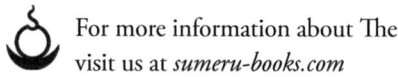

For more information about The Sumeru Press
visit us at *sumeru-books.com*

UNDERSTANDING THE TIBETAN BUDDHIST TEMPLE
A photographic study of Vajrayana shrine offerings
John Harvey Negru

Foreword Page 7

Part I Page 9
A Garland of Precious Offerings to Enrich the Mind

Part II Page 79
The Golden Rosary of Karma Kargyu Lineage Holders

Part III Page 105
The Consecration of Dzambhala

Dedications Page 125

With the wish to free all sentient beings,
I take refuge at all times
in the Buddha, Dharma and Sangha
until the attainment of full Enlightenment.

Today, in the presence of the Enlightened Ones,
inspired by compassion, wisdom and joyous effort,
I generate the mind aspiring for full Buddhahood
for the sake of all living beings.

For as long as space endures
and for as long as sentient beings remain,
until then may I too abide
to dispel the misery of the world.

His Holiness the Dalai Lama
Beneath the Bodhi Tree in Bodh Gaya, India
February 14, 1980

This is said to be the exact location where Shakyamuni Buddha achieved Enlightenment. The tree is a direct descendent of the original tree growing there more than 2500 years ago.

FOREWORD

This small book is an annotated collection of photographs of statues, shrine offerings, paintings, and other objects at Karma Tekchen Zabsal Ling, a Vajrayana Buddhist Temple in Aurora, Ontario. The temple is affiliated with the Thrangu lineage and is part of the Karma Kargyu school of Tibetan Buddhism. The photographs were taken over multiple sessions between 2008 and 2018. KTZL is under the auspices of HH the 17th Karmapa and it is also the home of Lama Tashi Dondup, a man of great gentleness and generosity.

In any Buddhist temple, the central focus is a statue of Shakyamuni, the historical Buddha. In a small Mahayana or Vajrayana chapel, one might instead have a statue or icon of a celestial Buddha such as Maitreya (the future Buddha), Amitabha (one of the five dhyani Buddhas), a Bodhisattva in peaceful or wrathful form (eg. Avalokitesvara/Hayagriva), or a Dharma Protector (eg. Mahakala).

However, in addition to these main statues and icons, one will invariably find other statues and smaller objects of spiritual significance on the shrine as well. The purpose of this book is to showcase and describe some of these secondary ritual objects, so as to give a fuller picture of Vajrayana iconography.

Part I focuses specifically on the shrine room and main shrine. Part II shows a series of paintings hanging around the shrine room perimeter, portraying the Kargyu lineage. Part III is a collection of photographs showing the consecration of a set of new statues for the temple, as well as some other items in a secondary chapel. Sanskrit terms are used, with Tibetan translations in brackets where relevant.

Religion is as much about the supporting concepts as it is about a central belief or faith. Images (in two or three dimensions) of central figures cannot convey all of those, even though they are tightly packed with symbolic significance. The images are too circumscribed by iconographic constraints. On the other hand, shrine offerings afford an opportunity to highlight ideas and values beyond the basics. They also provide a gateway for practitioners by delighting the senses and engaging them on a visceral level.

Vajrayana Buddhist shrines often display what are known as the eight auspicious offerings: water for drinking, water for washing, flowers, incense, lights, perfumes, food and musical instruments. These are represented in symbolic form as a row of bowls of water or lamps or in the form of a mandala offering.

In Vajrayana ceremonies, these offerings are also invoked through prayer, mantra (ritual words) and mudra (ritual gestures). More elaborate versions of short and long mandala offerings are rituals that are frequently incorporated into larger ceremonies.

Shrine offerings display great creativity in their conception and making. From an artistic point of view, they reveal much of interest about the culture from which they spring. However, this is secondary to their purpose as focii for aspiration.

In the Vajrayana (tantric Buddhism) the spiritual power of things is manifest in their agency. Ritual objects are used as tools and as vehicles of practice. As such, their activity may be directed to human participants in a ritual, or to beings in other realms who may affect or be affected by the event. As such, they are serious business, not merely pretty acoutrements. Tibetan hagiographies are replete with stories of yogis who accomplished miracles such as astral travel to other worlds, splitting mountains, subduing demons and so on – through the proper use of ritual objects.

In the west, we tend to recast those stories in psychological terms in order to make their meaning accessible to us. That is an excellent beginning. But to understand how those stories work within the cultures that gave birth to them is another matter. For that, an attitude of respect and an open heart are needed.

I have been fortunate in meeting and studying with a number of Vajrayana teachers, beginning with the Venerable Kalu Rinpoche in 1972, and I am eternally grateful to them for nurturing my understanding through the years that have followed.

I would especially like to thank His Holiness the 14th Dalai Lama, His Holiness the 16th Karmapa, Tara Tulku Rinpoche, Panchen Otrul Rinpoche, Kyabgon Chetsang Rinpoche, and Zasep Tulku Rinpoche, as well as Kalu Rinpoche. Thank you too, to the many other Buddhist teachers, monks, and nuns whose example continues to be an inspiration long after our meeting.

This small book is one of a series of mandala offerings I have made and will make unendingly to thank them for their incomparable kindness. My goal in presenting this offering is manifold. May it purify my bodhi mandala and increase my skill in means. May it please my teachers. May it inspire others in their spiritual journey along the Path of Seeing. And may it document a small part of the richness of Buddhism in Canada.

OM IDAM GURU RATNA MANDALAKAM NIRYATAYAMI
OM ARGHAM PADYAM PUSHPE DHUPE ALOKE GANDHE NAIVIDYA SHABDA HUM SVA HA

John Harvey Negru [Karma Yonten Gyatso] Ottawa, 2018

Part 1

A Garland of Precious Offerings to Enrich the Mind

Karma Tekchen Zabsal Ling, Toronto Thrangu Centre, Ontario
Aurora, Ontario, Canada

This is the main shrine room of the temple, from about halfway back in the hall.

Shakyamuni Buddha

Gilded metal, about six feet in height.

Shakyamuni, the historical Buddha, is represented here in the "Calling the Earth to Witness" pose, with his left hand in meditation holding a begging bowl and his right hand touching the ground.

Surrounding him is an aura, which can be interpreted variously as representing the union of emptiness and bliss, the union of wisdom and compassion, or an emanation of his holiness.

The statue is draped with an orange silk robe, reminiscent of the robes worn by monks.

Draped around the begging bowl is a traditional Tibetan offering scarf (*khata*) woven with symbols of the eight auspicious offerings. In this site, various crystals have been placed in the bowl.

Above him is a royal parasol. To the left and right are victory banners (*gyaltsen*) hanging from the ceiling.

Shakyamuni is often depicted flanked by two of his leading disciples, Ananda and Mahakasyapa.

In front of the base are portraits of His Holiness the Dalai Lama and His Holiness the Karmapa.

Before these are an array of other offerings.

The main shrine room, left side

The Altar and Shrine Room

The main shrine room, right side

14 Understanding the Tibetan Buddhist Temple

The altar

The Altar and Main Statue 15

Shakyamuni, flanked by Ananda on his right and Mahakasyapa on his left

Ananda
Ananda was Shakyamuni's cousin and one of his ten principal disciples. Most of the sutras of the Sutta Pitaka are attributed to his remarkable recollection of the Buddha's teachings. He was known as the Guardian of the Dharma.

Mahakasyapa
One of Shakyamuni's closest disciples. He was a master ascetic, and assumed leadership of the Sangha after the Buddha's death. In Mahayana Buddhism, he is considered the First Patriarch.

The altar

A side view showing the relative prominence of its various planes.

The left alcoves
The two main alcoves house Dzambhala (left) and Mahakala (right). Directly below Dzambhala are two curtained alcoves housing wrathful energies. To the right of them are two alcoves housing offerings to the animal realm. Surrounding these six alcoves are six alcoves housing statatues of Tara. Across the top and down the far left are nine alcoves of sutras.

The right alcoves
The main alcove houses Tara (*Drolma*), the female Buddha known as the Mother of Liberation. Surrounding her are fourteen alcoves housing statatues of Tara. Together, these are the twenty-one emanations of Tara traditionally honoured in Vajrayana Buddhism. Across the top and down the far left are nine alcoves of sutras.

**His Holiness
The XIVth Dalai Lama**

Head of the Tibetan Buddhist religion and former titular head of state for Tibet in exile (having resigned in 2011). He is recognized as the incarnation of Avalokitesvara, the Bodhisattva of Compassion.

The present Dalai Lama was born in Tibet in 1935 but fled to India after the Communist Chinese invasion in 1956. He is a refugee.

In front of the portrait is a small Nirvana stupa (*chorten*).

His Holiness
The XVIIth Karmapa

Head of the Kargyu lineage of Tibetan Buddhism.

The Gyalwa Karmapas were the first lamas in Tibet to be recognized by reincarnation. The current Karmapa was born in eastern Tibet in 1985, but in 1999 fled to India, where he now studies with HH the Dalai Lama.

In front of the portrait is a small gilded copper statue of Amitayus (*Tsepame*).

Stupa
Also known as a chorten in Tibetan

There are eight styles of stupas:
- Lotus Blossom
- Enlightenment
- Many Doors
- Descent from Tushita Heaven
- Great Miracles
- Reconciliation
- Complete Victory
- Nirvana

The stupa is a visual symbol of the mind of the Buddha. In the ceremony of making offerings to the teacher and requesting him or her to turn the wheel of the Dharma, three offerings are made – torma ritual cakes representing the body of the Buddha, a sutra representing the speech of the Buddha, and a stupa representing the mind of the Buddha.

The design of a stupa is a microcosmic representation of the universe, with Mount Sumeru in the middle. The four elements (earth, water, fire, air) are represented, as are the thirteen levels of Bodhisattva training, the sun and moon, the all-seeing eyes of the Buddha, and so on.

This is a particularly fine metal specimen, about ten inches high.

According to Khandro.net, "Lama Tashi Dondup [the resident teacher at KTZL] is one of the few acknowledged specialists in matters relating to the visual supports used for Tibetan Buddhist practice, from tormas to thangkas, mandalas and stupas. He was the consultant and manager for the erection of the 16th Karmapa's stupa in Crestone, Colorado, among others."

Amitayus
Buddha of Infinite Life

Amitayus (*Tsepame*) is an alternate manifestation of Amitabha (*Opame*), the Buddha of Infinite Light, who presides in the Western Paradise of Sukhavati (*Dewachen*). In this form, he is portrayed in meditation, holding a vase of elixir. (Portrayed as Amitabha, he is not holding the vase.)

He is one of the Five Dhyani [Celestial or Meditation] Buddhas along with Vairocana, Ratnasambhava, Amoghasiddhi, and Akshobya. Dhyani Buddhas and Bodhisattvas are distinguished by their royal finery, including crowns, necklaces, earrings, bracelets, anklets, and flowing elaborate garments.

This specimen is about eight inches high, cast in copper, with gilded and polychrome highlights, and inset with semi-precious stones.

Consecrated statues such as this are sealed with written prayers, relics and other small offerings inside the base.

Virtually all high-quality metal Buddhist statues in the Vajrayana style originate in Nepal, where the metalwork tradition stretches back for centuries.

Auspicious offerings

This small compilation, made of painted wood and about twelve inches wide, sits directly below the main statue of Shakyamuni. It represents a variety of auspicious offerings. Such offerings frequently depict what are known as the seven possessions of the universal monarch (a rhinoceros horn, the square earrings of the minster, a branch of precious coral, the round earrings of the queen, the insignia of the general, a pair of elephant tusks, and a triple-eyed gem enclosed in a trefoil gold mount). These seven symbols represent the seven components of the mandala offering.

<u>Front row</u>: 13 aspiration jewels, representing the 13 levels of Mahayana Buddhist training for Bodhisattvas
<u>Second row</u>: 4 elephant tusks (a royal offering); 10 aspiration jewels
<u>Third row</u>: Eternity fruit; coral; 3 aspiration jewels; heavenly peaches
<u>Fourth row</u>: Mirror; conch; coral; treasure vases
<u>Fifth row</u>: 5 treasure vases surrounding 6 flaming commitment jewels (representing the 6 senses). Commitment jewels in wrathful representations are plucked eyeballs, held by deities who have conquered the passions and completed the Path of Seeing.

Auspicious offerings

On the lower level are seven bowls of water, refilled each morning. They represent:

- Water for drinking
- Water for washing
- Flowers
- Lights
- Incense
- Food
- Music

When you see lamas performing a series of mudras during a ceremony, these are often gestural representations for the seven offerings.

On the second level are five lights. On the upper level are a Long Life Medicine Buddha Vase, draped in blue, two lights, a vase of flowers, and a prayer wheel. Just to the left, you can see one of another series of seven oil lamp bowls. Like the water bowls, these are tended to each morning.

Incense Offerings

These are seven incense offerings in glass bowls of coloured rice, sitting directly at the base of the main statue of Shakyamuni. The incense sticks are interlaced, in a pattern reminiscent of the eternal knot. Behind the incense in each bowl is a coloured paper cut-out bouquet of lotuses. Behind them, on an upper level, are seven torma offering cakes. They're not actually edible. They may be made made of tsampa barley flour or plaster, and they are painted for permanency. Each torma features 35 aspiration jewels as offerings to the 35 Confession Buddhas, elephant tusks, and flowers. They are about fifteen inches tall.

Incense Offering

Another variant, using sticks of incense wrapped in paper. The paper on the lowest ring is ornamented with lotus petals. The second ring shows the eight auspicious symbols. The third ring shows the seven auspicious possessions of the univeral monarch, the fourth ring shows green Tara, the Saviouress. The top ring shows a collection of aspiration jewels.

There are many varieties of Tibetan incense, known for their earthy and herbal scents.

Typical ingredients include aromatic woods such as juniper, cedar, and sandalwood, as well as myrrh, amber, frankincense, snow lotus herb, hibiscus, saffron, red orpine, clove, borneol, camphor, or Cordyceps fungus. Recipes vary according to purpose; for example, medicinal incense is more likely to contain camphor or Cordyceps.

The ingredients are bound together with Tragacanth powder, which forms a paste when mixed with water.

Mandala Offerings

Each of these mandala offerings is about ten inches high

To make a mandala offering, one begins with a clean plate, which one then ritually cleans by rubbing it clockwise three times with a cloth. One then rubs it counter-clockwise three times to imbue it with all good qualities.

Then as one performs the visualization ritual, one pours rice into the rings symbolically at various points in the prayer. On a golden ground, surrounded by an iron vajra fence, is Mount Sumeru, surrounded by the four continents. One offers the precious mountain, the wish-granting cow, the unploughed harvest, the precious wheel, queen, minister, elephant, horse, general and treasure vase. Next one offers the goddesses of garlands, song, dance, flowers, incense, light and perfume. Then come offerings of the sun, moon, precious parasol and banner of victory in all directions. The centre finial is the offering of All Good, with nothing missed or impure.

Making 100,000 mandala offerings is one of the Foundation Practices (*Ngondro*) of Vajrayana Buddhism.

Mandala Offerings

Mount Sumeru Extensive Offering Mandala
Cast and repoussé yellow metal, approximately 24 inches wide and 30 inches high. This is an extremely unusual piece with many different components.

It is based on Chogyal Pakpa's Thirty-Seven Point Manadala Offering. In the centre is a representation of Mount Sumeru as a celestial pavilion, surrounded by the four continents. Our world, Jambudvipa, is the southern continent, the direction seen on the opposite page. Above are the west and east perspectives.

The offerings include: the precious mountain; the wish-granting tree; the cow that unceasingly gives milk; the crop that needs no sowing; the seven precious emblems of royalty (golden wheel, wish-granting jewel, queen, minister, elephant, horse, general); the treasure vase; the eight offering goddesses (of beauty, garlands, song, dance, flowers, incense, light, perfume); the sun; the moon; the precious umbrella; and the banner of victory in all directions.

In less elaborate mandala offerings, the elements are visualized. Here they are visibly recreated: once seen, never forgotten.

Mandala Offerings 31

Offerings to the Wrathful Ones

On the two lower levels are offering bowls and lights. Above them are offerings to the Wrathful Deities.

At the far left is the Dzambhala arrow, bedecked with five-coloured pennants.

To the right of that is a torma offering to Hayagriva (*Tamzin*), the Wrathful form of Avalokitesvara. On top of the torma is a small card (known as a tsakli card) depicting Hayagriva.

To the right of that is a large torma offering to Padmasambhava, the Buddhist guru who brought Vajrayana Buddhism to Tibet in the 9th century CE after subduing the demons there. He is shown in the tsakli card at the top.

Towards the far right is a ritual initiation vase (*bumpa*), with a tsakli card of Hayagriva on it, a red cloth cover, and a stopper decorated with a peacock feather finial. This would be used for distributing blessed water during a Hayagriva Empowerment.

In ritual practice, the deity is represented by the torma, imbued with his or her presence. Peaceful tormas are typically white, while wrathful tormas are typically red. The specifics of design depend on the deity represented.

Large Hayagriva Torma

A more elaborate version, seen closer.

Large Padmasambhava Torma

Padmasambhava, the Lotus Born One, is represented here by a wrathful torma with a lotus petal base. The torma shape is in the style of a Heaped Lotus Stupa.

Above, in a wish-fulfilling tree, are lotus, sun, and moon discs, and the seed syllable HAM, representing Acala, a Dharma Protector (also popular in Japan, where he is called Fudo Myoo). Above that is a wrathful offering of six commitment jewels engulfed in flames. Padmasambhava is shown in the tsakli card at the top.

Resting on the shelf behind the smaller torma on the right, you can just see the edge of a tsakli card depicting Acala, who is blue. Acala is considered especially powerful in burning away impurities that obstruct one's path to Enlightenment.

Wrathful Offerings

In the centre is a blue Mahakala (*Gonpo*) torma flanked by two ritual skull cups.

The skull torma on the far left represents transformation of impure body, speech, and mind, into the Buddha's body, speech, and mind. It is also a *memento mori*, reminding us of the brevity of human life.

The alcoves behind are filled with a large collection of animal figurines, wrathful tormas, and small offerings of candy, trinkets, and so on.

Torma

A peaceful torma on the left and a semi-wrathful torma on the right.

Both show heaps of offerings of aspiration jewels flanked by elephant tusks on the base level, in bowls of rice sprinked with semi-precious stones.

This red, wrathful torma is dedicated to Acala. Peaceful tormas are usually white with a round conical form. Tormas for wrathful deities are usually red with sculpted triangular flames at their tops. Note the offering candies at the base. The Acala tsakli card shows him in blue with a skull head, holding a skull cup and flaying knife.

Torma

This large, elaborate torma is on the right (peaceful) side, when facing the altar. It is about twenty inches high, and in a plexiglass case to keep it in good shape. The alcoves above it are dedicated to Tara, the Saviouress.

Tormas can be extremely elaborate. As offerings, they may remain on the shrine. As a matter of expediency, such tormas, made of more durable material and varnished, are common in this place and time.

Other forms of tormas are used in offering ceremonies where they are intended for disposal after ritual use. They were traditionally made from barley flour, butter and sugar.

They are offered and consecrated. Once used in such a service, they are deemed to have absorbed the energies awakened in the ceremony and are left outside to be devoured by animals, hungry ghosts and hell beings. Sometimes the torma is left outside the door; sometimes it is thrown in a nearby body of water or river.

One such ritual occurs on half-moon nights. Known as a Tsok Offering, or tantric feast, it includes elaborate food and drink offerings which are consecrated and then shared by the participants. At the end of the ceremony, a portion of the offerings are put out along with torma offerings for the benefit of those in the lower realms.

When flour tormas are being used as offerings to wrathful deities, they are made without sugar and may contain other ingredients as well, such as black sesame seeds. In this instance, their purpose is to absorb all negative energies and remove obstructions to practice. After use they may be burned in a ritual fire offering.

Kapala

Skull cup, used to hold amrita (sacred nectar) during pujas (ceremonies). This kapala is gilded metal, about six inches high.

Amrita is usually water consecrated with saffron and honey. Other ingredients may be added or substituted depending on the specific ritual being performed.

The lid is opened at appropriate points in the service. Amrita may or may not be distributed, depending on whether the offering is being made to the Buddhas and Bodhisattvas, with a request that it be purified, transformed and increased, or whether it is subsequently being offered to the congregants.

The skull shape refers to the transitory nature of human existence. It also refers to the seriousness with which one must approach spiritual practice. In earlier times, the actual skull of a highly respected religious teacher might have been used, but such kapalas are obviously extremely rare.

The lid is topped with a vajra (*dorje*), the thunderbolt of spiritual power.

To the left, one can see a portion of the handle of the spoon used to distribute the amrita.

Implements for Wrathful Tantric Rituals

Phurbu

The ritual dagger has a three-sided blade, and the handle is decorated with wrathful deities, topped by a vajra finial.

The phurbu is used to subdue demons who would obstruct the teaching and practice of Buddhism.

In the phurbu ritual, demons are summoned before the Buddha by one of the wrathful Dharma Protectors and forced to stand in triangular holes around the mandala. Phurbus are then driven down through their heads, immobilizing them and commiting them to uphold the Dharma.

The base of the dagger on the left is decorated with skulls.

The phurbu on right is made of iron, perhaps from a meteor. Meteor iron is known as sky metal, and is considered extremexly auspicious for potency.

Dadar Arrow and Treasure Vase

These embody prayers for prosperity. The dadar arrow is a ritual instrument used in many Long Life practices for recalling all the aspects of our vital energy and protective energy that are damaged, lost or stolen.

The arrow is wrapped in ribbons of five colours, symbolizing the five Buddha Families. It is about eighteen inches long. The vase contains a small quantity of money and jewels.

These are located on the far left corner of the shrine, dedicated to Dzambhala, who is the Dharma Protector associated with wealth. Their placement there indicates that Dzambhala's role is not central, but important in its place. The alcove dedicated to Dzambhala is above and to the right, just outside the frame.

In the alcove behind them, you can see some wood-block sutra books wrapped in cloth.

Prayer Wheel

This is an electric model, about eight inches tall. It contains 800,000 *Om Mani Padme Hum* mantras inside a printed tin drum that spins. It is manufactured by the Global Fun Company in Guangdong, China. It sells in Canada for about $95.00.

The decorations on the tin, from bottom to top, are lotus petals, auspicious offerings, the eight auspicious symbols, the mantra, and a victory banner.

It is on the far right side of the altar base.

Prayer wheels of all sizes are a common sight in Vajrayana countries. There are even small, solar-powered versions made for car dashboards. Spinning them is considered equivalent to repeating all the mantras inside with each turn.

Statue of Milarepa

Gilded metal, about four inches tall.

Milarepa is the beloved 11th-century yogi who captured the essence of Buddhism in 100,000 spiritual songs, many of which are extant today.

He is regarded as one of the founders of the Karma Kargyu lineage.

He is always depicted in a non-monastic yogi's robe, which is all he needed to wear during the harsh Tibetan winters, thanks to his yogic abilities. His right hand is to his ear hearing the sound of truth. He is holding a skullcup, symbolic of of transient existence, and sitting on an antelope skin (the traditional iconographic throne cover for the Bodhisattva of Compassion).

Amitayus
Buddha of Infinite Life

This is an alternate form, about six inches tall. It has been cast in bronze, but not gilded, painted, or enhanced with inset stones. He is one of the Long Life Deities of Vajrayana Buddhism.

The statue is shown here in front of the portrait of His Holiness the 17th Karmapa. In the photo of the full portrait [page 21], taken on another occasion, a different, more finished Amitayus statue is in this spot.

Bumpa Offering Vase
Repoussé copper, about twelve inches high.

Bumpas are used to pour water into offering bowls on the shrine or for ritual cleansing of the mouth before initiations. During initiations they may also be used to distribute amrita nectar.

This specimen displays a heavily-worked assortment of traditional motifs: dragon spout and phoenix handle; lotus base; flaming aspiration jewel finial; eternal knot spout support; and eight auspicious symbol flask.

Opposite page >
Two bumpas, decorated with Medicine Buddha tsakli cards
On the left, repoussé white metal, about twelve inches high, with a blue crocheted cloth and a peacock feather finial. On the right, brass with a white khata and a kusa grass finial.

Kusa grass is often used in Vajrayana initiations. It is the type of grass that Shakyamuni used as his meditation cushion on the night of his Enlightenment. During longer initiations, short and long pieces are distributed to initiants between the second and third day, to place under their pillows and mattresses respectively, to enhance their dreams, which are interpreted on the third day as part of the ceremony.

Ritual Vases 45

Offerings to the animal realm

The alcove on the left contains animals we mostly use, eat, or treat as pets. The alcove on the right contains animals we mostly fear. In addition to the small replicas of animals are a selection of wrathful, semi-wrathful, and wrathful torma cakes. The alcoves also contain a variety of trinkets, candy, and other offerings.

Green Tara
The Saviouress

Tara (*Drolma*) is a female Buddha. One of her Bodhisattva Vows was that when she attained Enlightenment, she would do so as a woman, showing that Buddhahood is gender-neutral.

She is much loved by Tibetans and figures prominently in both Vajrayana iconography and ritual.

In practice, she is represented as having twenty-one different manifestations, of which Green Tara is the most common.

Her right hand is in the gesture of bestowing the gift of liberation from the eight great fears, while her left hand is at her heart in the gesture of bestowing refuge. In each hand she holds the stem of an utpala flower. She sits on a lotus throne, with her right leg out as she steps down into the world. A lotus bud rises up to cushion her foot.

This statue is gilded copper, standing about thirty inches high. As with many statues on Vajrayana altars, it is clothed in a fancy brocade. It resides in the main alcove on the right side of the altar.

Red Tara
Drolma Barvai Odcan, the "Tara Who Averts the Enemies and Mantra's Spell" who is red like the fire at the end of the eon, sits on blue lotus, and holds a crossed vajra

Another of the twenty-one Taras, seen here in one of the smaller alcoves. Each of the twenty Taras other than Green Tara is identified by their holding a flower, with a specific symbol on it. They may also appear in wrathful fom.

In this gilded copper statue, about eighteen inches high, the lotus in Tara's left hand is surmounted by a crossed vajra (visvavajra in Sanskrit). According to Rigpa Shedra, the crossed vajra "symbolizes the principle of absolute stability.

"In the cosmographic description of Mount Meru a vast crossed vajra supports and underlies the entire physical universe. Similarly in the representation of the mandala, a vast crossed vajra serves as the immoveable support or foundation of the mandala palace…."

The crossed vajras symbol is also marked on the plates sealing the bases of consecrated statues.

Yellow Tara
Namgyalma, the "Victorious Lady," the "One Who Has Accomplished Immortality"

In this statue, the lotus in Tara's left hand is surmounted by a Long Life Vase. Yellow represents the enlightened activity of increasing the positive qualities conducive to a long life, peace, happiness and success in one's Dharma practice.

Golden Tara
Yangchenma, the "Treasure of Wisdom," the "Lady with a shining face like an array of hundred autumn full moons"

In this statue, the lotus in Tara's left hand is surmounted by a Mirror Increasing Abundance.

Opposite page >
Avalokitesvara Bodhisattva with a Thousand Hands and a Thousand Eyes

During another of my visits to KTZL, the main Tara statue had been removed from its alcove and replaced with this large statue of Avalokitesvara.

Avalokitesvara, the Bodhisattva of Compassion

Thousand-Handed, Thousand-Eyed Avalokitesvara Bodhisattva
The Bodhisattva Who Hears the Sounds of the World

It is said that when Avalokitesvara, the Bodhisattva of Compassion, saw the world's suffering, his head exploded in grief.

He grew a thousand arms to help beings in all realms, and each hand was endowed with an eye to see how best to help.

These pictures were taken when the statue was in an auxiliary chapel containing (as yet undedicated) memorial plaques for the the dead.

As with the more common representation of Avalokitesvara (*Chenresigs*), the main four arms are in the traditional gestures. The centre arms hold a wish-fulfilling jewel in a prayerful position. The main right hand holds a rosary and the main left hand holds a lotus.

He is also holding a Dharma Wheel a lower right hand and a human thigh bone in a lower left hand. His lowermost right hand is in the gesture of bestowing the gift of liberation with the all-seeing eye. His lowermost left hand is holding a Long Life Vase.

The various faces and their colours refer to the five Buddha families. Since Avalokitesvara is of the Amitabha family, Amitabha is shown as the top head.

The statue is painted ceramic, about forty inches tall, on a copper lotus base.

Two-Armed Mahakala
Principal Dharma Protector of the Karma Kargyu Lineage and specifically of His Holiness the Karmapa

The two-armed manifestation is also known as the Black Cloak Mahakala. He is represented as standing on two human corpses.

According to Himalayan Art Resources: "The fiercely wrathful, Black Cloak Mahakala is black in colour, with one face, three round bulbous eyes, a large gaping red mouth with bared white fangs. His yellow beard, eyebrows and hair flow upward like flames. The right hand holds aloft a curved flaying knife with a vajra handle. The left holds a white blood-filled skullcup to the heart. Adorned with a crown of five dry white skulls, earrings, bracelets and a garland of freshly severed heads, he wears a great black cloak as his unique characteristic. He stands surrounded by black smoke and red licks of the flames of pristine awareness fire."

Folklore has it that Mahakala's face is swollen and lumpy because Karma Pakshi, the second Karmapa, once slapped him for being late when summoned.

The statue is gilded and painted copper, about thirty inches high.

Opposite page <
Palden Lhamo

Palden Lhamo is considered the patroness protector of Tibet, and (in a different manifestation) especially of the Dalai Lama lineage.

She is the only female Dharma Protector, and Mahakala's consort. In her left hands she holds a sceptre and an archer's bow. In her right hands she holds a flaying knife extended, and a phurba dagger at her heart.

The mule she rides on has an eye on its left rump where her angry husband's arrow hit it after she killed her son (who was destined, and being raised, to be the one to finally put an end to Buddhism) and used his skin as a saddle blanket. The poisoned arrow was intended for her but missed. She healed the wound and transformed it into a wisdom eye.

The statue is gilded copper, about twelve inches tall, and sits at Mahakala's right knee.

Right
Dark Red Tara
Jigyed Chenmo, the "Great Terrifying Lady"

Unlike the peaceful Tara manifestations in other altar alcoves, this one in an alcove near Mahakala is in half-wrathful form. Like Mahakala, she wears a five-skull crown and a flaming halo. She bears her teeth but does not extend her tongue. In her hands, she holds a phurba dagger at her heart. Like the peaceful Taras, she sits with one leg partially extended, resting on a lotus.

Dorje Legpa
Dharma Protector, the "Oath-Bound"

At Mahakala's left knee is a statue of Dorje Legpa, another Dharma Protector, riding a goat with twisted horns.

He is especially associated with protecting Mahamudra (*Dzogchen*) teachings and treasure teachings.

In this rendition, he is swinging a varja axe in his right hand above his head, and holding a severed human heart in his left at his waist. Sometimes he is shown riding a Snow Lion and brandishing a varja instead of a varja axe. His also sometimes portrayed with a wide-brimmed metal hat.

  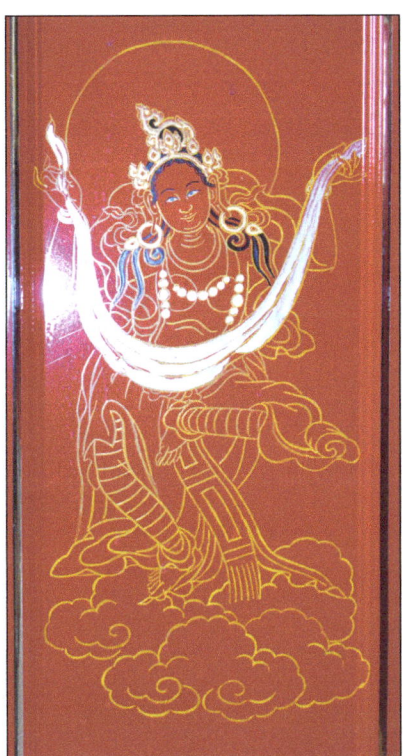 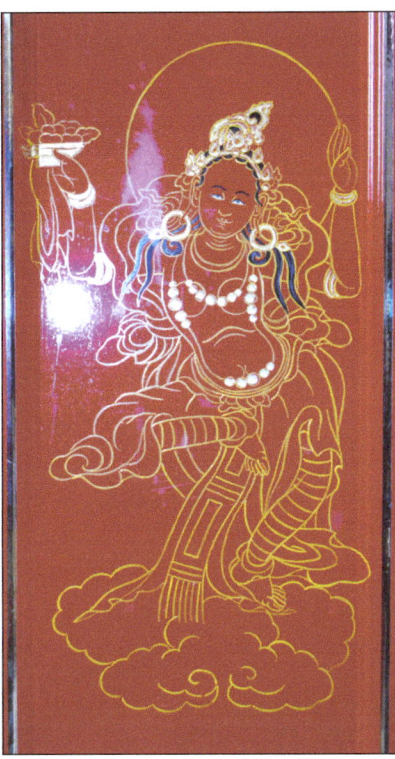

Heavenly Offering Maidens
Apsaras

These four maidens are drawn on the door panels of the altar base on the right side under the Tara alcoves.

Apsaras, or heavenly nymphs, are a motif depicted all over the Hindu and Buddhist world. Here, they are in the Tibetan style, dancing and offering a mirror, incense, a khata scarf, and a bowl of flowers.

The Very Venerable Thrangu Rinpoche
Portrait on teaching throne

VV Thrangu Rinpoche is the lineage patron of this temple.

This is a traditional teaching throne – a raised platform upon which high-ranking lamas preside over services and teachings. The pulpit in front is covered with brocade hangings, surmounted by a khata offering scarf.

When the presiding lama is not present, a portrait is usually substituted as an *aide de memoire*.

In front of the portrait is a repoussé and cloisonné representation of the wheel of Dharma. Beside it is a brass and golden kapala.

Opposite page >
Lectern
Shown without brocade cover

The main motif shows two deer flanking a Dharma Wheel, symbolic of Shakyamuni's first teaching in the Deer Park at Sarnath. Below is a row of lotus blossoms and garlands. Across the top are the Eight Auspicious Symbols:
- Victory Banner
- Pair of Golden Fish
- Long Life Vase
- Lotus Flower
- Conch
- Endless Knot
- Royal Parasol
- Dharma Wheel

Across the top is a frieze of lotus petals.

62 Understanding the Tibetan Buddhist Temple

Throne back detail
Carved and painted wood motifs of The Eight Auspicious Symbols.

Opposite page <
Throne back
Everthing that is offered is of the highest possible quality.

The Thousand Buddhas
Shakyamuni and Dzambhala

It is traditional in Buddhist temples from many different countries to have alcoves around the upper perimeter of the shrine room, filled with small Buddha statues. The statues are usually Shakyamuni or Amitabha. Sometimes the number is poetically exaggerated to ten thousand.

The significance of the number of Buddha statues is twofold:

- It was foretold that there would be a thousand Buddhas in the Auspicious Age, in which we live
- Buddha Nature is integral to each of us and we all have the potential to awaken this Enlightenment

In this particular instance, the statues of Dzambhala, a Dharma Protector associated with prosperity, are an auspicious addition.

The Thousand Buddhas

Dorje and Bell

These are the quintessential ritual implements of Vajrayana Buddhism. The vajra (*dorje*), the thunderbolt of spiritual power, is held in the right hand. The bell (*ghanta* in Sanskrit), whose sound is the essence of wisdom, is held in the left. During ceremonies, they are used in choreographed hand gestures (*mudra* in Sanskrit) to symbolically represent ideas being expressed through recitation or mental visualization.

These ritual implements are covered in motifs with many meanings, and are perhaps the most widely recognized symbols of Tibetan Buddhism. However, they can also be found in tantric traditions as far away as the Indonesian island of Bali.

They are shown here with a small hand drum (*damaru* in Sanskrit) used in tantric rituals (held in the right hand along with the vajra). Damaru of all kinds are traditionally paired with a long sash or tail called a chopen.

Percussion Instruments
Cymbals, bowl gong, wooden fish

Buddhist chanting is typically close to monotone, but accompanied by a rich variety of percussion instruments. Cymbals and gongs are used periodically for emphasis, while the wooden fish (a hollowed-out spherical gourd shape) is struck repeatedly with a padded mallet to keep the beat.

Each seat is covered with a Tibetan rug.

68   Understanding the Tibetan Buddhist Temple

Brass and Woodwinds

Long and short horns, shawms

On the opposite page, we see a long horn (shown close-up on this page). It has a trumpet-style mouthpiece and produces a low tone. Under the table on the right, we see two smaller horns in the same style, serving the same function as thigh bone trumpets seen in paintings of yogis engaged in tantric rituals.

On this page, we see a pair of shawms, double-reed woodwinds with finger holes to obtain a scale of notes. The sound is like an oboe, but played in the upper register.

Tibetan music, while harsh to Western sensibilities, is undeniably moving. Its purpose is as much to awaken and direct supernatural energies as it is to accompany human voices.

Drums

Chanting during rituals is often accompanied by drum beats. This drum frame features a dream cloud motif along the top brace, topped by a flaming aspiration jewel set on a lotus and flanked by dragons. It is one of a pair.

The cord holding the drum is braided into an eternal knot using cords of five colours (red, blue, green, white and yellow – symbolizing the five celestial Buddhas).

The drumstick holders are decorated with tassels featuring knots and ceramic balls.

Opposite page >
Other Drums

Two additional drum stands at the back of the shrine room. One has a Dharma wheel flanked by deer as the finial, while the other has a dream cloud with aspiration jewels.

Musical Instruments 71

Recitation texts for ceremonies
Sadhanas (practice manuals) for pujas (ceremonies)

These small booklets contain verses, mantras, and occasionally pictures. They are used in ritual recitations on a regular cycle.

In the traditional style of Tibetan books, they are short but wide. In days of old, they would have been printed from woodblocks. This style originated in India, where books were scribed on palm leaves. Now, they are photocopied and spiral-bound. However, it is worth noting that the world's oldest book printed with moveable type is a copy of *The Diamond Sutra* found in the Mogao Caves in Dunhuang, China, dated to 868 CE.

Since these books were originally unbound sheaves of pages, they would be wrapped in cloth for protection. These cloths, known as pecha covers, could be quite elaborate.

The Buddhist canon is quite vast, containing sutras (known as the Kanjur) and commentaries (known as the Tanjur).

On the opposite page, we see a sadhana book, a Tanjur text in its red pecha cover, surmounted by an amber rosary, sitting on a shrine room desk, and a collection of Kanjur texts in elaborate pecha covers, sitting in alcoves on the altar.

Texts are treated with reverence since they are created for spiritual purposes rather than entertainment. One would not put them on the floor, sit on them, or step over them. They are never thrown in the garbage and specific rituals are involved in their disposal.

Furthermore, because of the nature of their content and use in tantric rituals, they are not freely available for anybody to read. Rather, one must have received the relevant initiation from a qualified teacher and that initiation would have included a Word empowerment along with the other empowerments associated with the particular Buddha, Bodhisattva, or Dharma Protector being invoked.

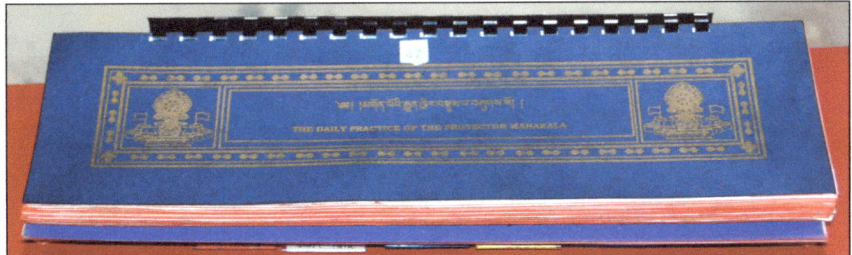

Fire Puja Implements
Variations on Vajra and Bell

This pair of implements is rather large. Each is about twelve inches long. They are intended for use in wrathful rituals.

Sang (Smoke) and Sur (Aroma) Fire Brazier

Fire rituals are another common component of Tibetan Buddhist ceremonies. This bronze brazier, about twelve feet high and decorated with dragons in the Chinese style, sits outside the front door of the temple. Such braziers are typically found in Chinese monasteries as incense burners outside the front doors.

Fragrant woods such as juniper and sandalwood are the most frequent substances burned, but other items such as ghee, black sesame seeds may be used for specific purposes.

A Manual of Ritual Fire Offerings, by Sharpa Tulku and Michael Perrott, published by the Library of Tibetan Works and Archives, Dharamsala, 1987, remains the definitive resource on this subject.

76 Understanding the Tibetan Buddhist Temple

Buddha Statues
in the Chinese style

Buddhist temples are often recipients of donated Buddha statues. This is a selection of small statues in plaster, ceramic, and metal. They were located in the memorial chapel. The bronze statues in the two upper pictures are Sai Nyingpo (Ksitigarbha), the ceramic statue is Kwan Yin (Avalokitesvara), the small bronze statue in the lower picture is Kuntuzangpo (Samantabhadra).

The small ball (about an inch in diameter) on a pedestal, shown here on the lower right, is known as a dragon pearl. You can also see one in the hands of the Ksitigarbha pictured above. The pearl is associated with spiritual energy, wisdom, prosperity, power, immortality, thunder, or the moon.

Offering Table
in the Chinese style

Offering tables are set up at the front of the shrine room. The officiant will face the altar and make offerings on behalf of the congregation. This table has been set up for a mandala offering and an incense offering.

    The table is Chinese, with dream cloud pattern brackets supporting the legs and bevelled ends. It is covered with an auspicious red runner, decorated with a motif of victory banners and stylized phoenix, and weighted with an end tassel.

Blessing Cord

In tantric initiations, participants usually receive blessing cords to wear around their necks afterwards as embodiments of their experiences. The cords are previously knotted – you can see the knot on the far left – and blown upon by the lama conducting the initiation. The prayers and breath embody all the spiritual power of the master being passed to the disciple. They are to be worn until the fall off.

In highest yoga tantra initiations, the cords may be used as protections during the ceremony, for which they are worn on the upper left arm.

Red is the colour usually used, but other colours associated with particular deities are sometimes used in association with their initiations.

Right >
Gyaltsen
Victory Banners

These colourful hangings decorate many Tibetan temples. They are reminiscent of the parasol, which is the royal symbol often found in icons and statues over the head of Shakyamuni Buddha.

The colours represent the five Buddha families: Vairocana – white; Ratnasambhava – yellow; Amitabha – red; Amoghasiddhi – green; Akshobya – blue.

Victory banner designs include the eight auspicious symbols, flowers, dragons, clouds, or other indigenous motifs. In the visualized three-dimensional mandala, victory banners represent architectural ornaments to the celestial mansion.

Part II

The Karma Kargyu Lineage
The Golden Rosary

ABOUT THE GOLDEN ROSARY

The Karma Kargyu lineage celebrated its 900th year in 2010, in a celebration known as the Kagyu Monlam.

In Buddhism, the unbroken, direct transmisson of the teaching from realized master to realized master is extremely important. In Vajrayana Buddhism, this transmission took the form of recognizing reincarnated high lamas at birth, and then "re-introducing" them to their previous standing through a childhood of study and practice with highly accomplished teachers. The Gyalwa Karmapa lineage was the first such lineage in Tibet, and it is known as the Golden Rosary.

The Golden Rosary reaches back beyond the First Karmapa to several important early teachers, and thence to Vajradhara (*Dorje Chang*), the primordial Buddha.

At Karma Tekchen Zabsal Ling, the shrine room is graced by a collection of thangka paintings of the lineage holders in the Golden Rosary. Some are the Karmapas, but the images also include leaders of the Shamarpa and Kenting Tai Situpa lineages who were responsible for discovering and training successive generations of Karmapas. Biographies of these great teachers are available elsewhere.

Each figure is identified by posture, gesture, garments, ritual implements, and other distinguishing features. Their retinues show their main students. Above them are the meditation deities (*Yidams*) of their personal practice, while below them are the meditation deities they are most closely associated with teaching. If you look closely at the paintings, you will also recognize many of the same elements found in the shrine room shown in Part I of this book, such as tormas, offering tables, bowls, lamps, sutra books, long life vases, stupas, phurbas, teaching thrones, brocades, and so on. A key element for identification are the implements held in the central figure's hands, such as vajra and bell, lotus, sutra book, or some other symbolic object, as well as the exact gesture of the hands. All these elements are iconic and very consistent across different portrayals of any particular teacher.

Also of particular note is the hat worn by each lineage holder. The Karma Kargyu is known as the Red Hat school. Hats for the Shamarpa, Situpa, and Gyaltsab are typically in the crown style: a central panel decorated with jewels under sun and moon, and side wings decorated with dream clouds. They are topped with finials. The hats for each of their lineages vary by the style of jewels and the direction in which the dream clouds trail. A variety of other hat styles can be seen in the paintings as well. Hats specific to other branches the Kagyu lineage (but not the Karma Kagyu), such as the Gampopa hat (worn by Kalu Rinpoche as representative of the Drikung Kagyu lineage, for example), are not shown here.

The Karmapa is shown wearing a black hat, known as the action crown. This hat is especially associated with the Karmapa lineage. The central panel features a crossed vajra under sun and moon, while the side wings feature dream clouds. The original black hat action crown was said to be a gift to the 2nd Karmapa from the heavenly tantric priestesses (*dakinis*), woven from their hair. In the Black Hat Initiation, the Karmapa meditates to become one with Avalokitesvara (*Chenresigs*), the Bodhisattva of Compassion, and after prayers by the congregation, he places the hat on his head, holding it with his right hand. To witness the ceremony is said to ensure one's attainment of the First Ground of a Bodhisattva within three lifetimes. His Holiness the 16th Karmapa performed the Black Hat Initiation in Toronto, at Deer Park United Church on St. Clair Avenue, in 1976. I was there.

The set of paintings you see here is a copy. The original set of paintings, known as the Sertreng collection, currently resides at Rumtek Monastery, Sikkim, India. They were presented as a gift to the 16th Karmapa in India in the 1960s by Sanggye Nyenpa Rinpoche who had commissioned the paintings in Kham, Tibet, prior to exile in India.

Each picture is captioned with the name and title of the subject. All dates are from the Common Era (CE). Some lineage holders were not hung in the shrine room for reasons of limited space, and I was not able to take pictures of them. Their names, but not their images, have been included here for completeness in identifying the lineage.

Vajradhara (Dorje Chang)
The Primordial Buddha

Tilopa
988–1069

The Golden Rosary 83

Naropa
?–1040

Marpa Chokyi Lodro
1012–1097

84 Understanding the Tibetan Buddhist Temple

Milarepa
1052–1135
Left and Opposite (close-up)

The Golden Rosary   85

86 Understanding the Tibetan Buddhist Temple

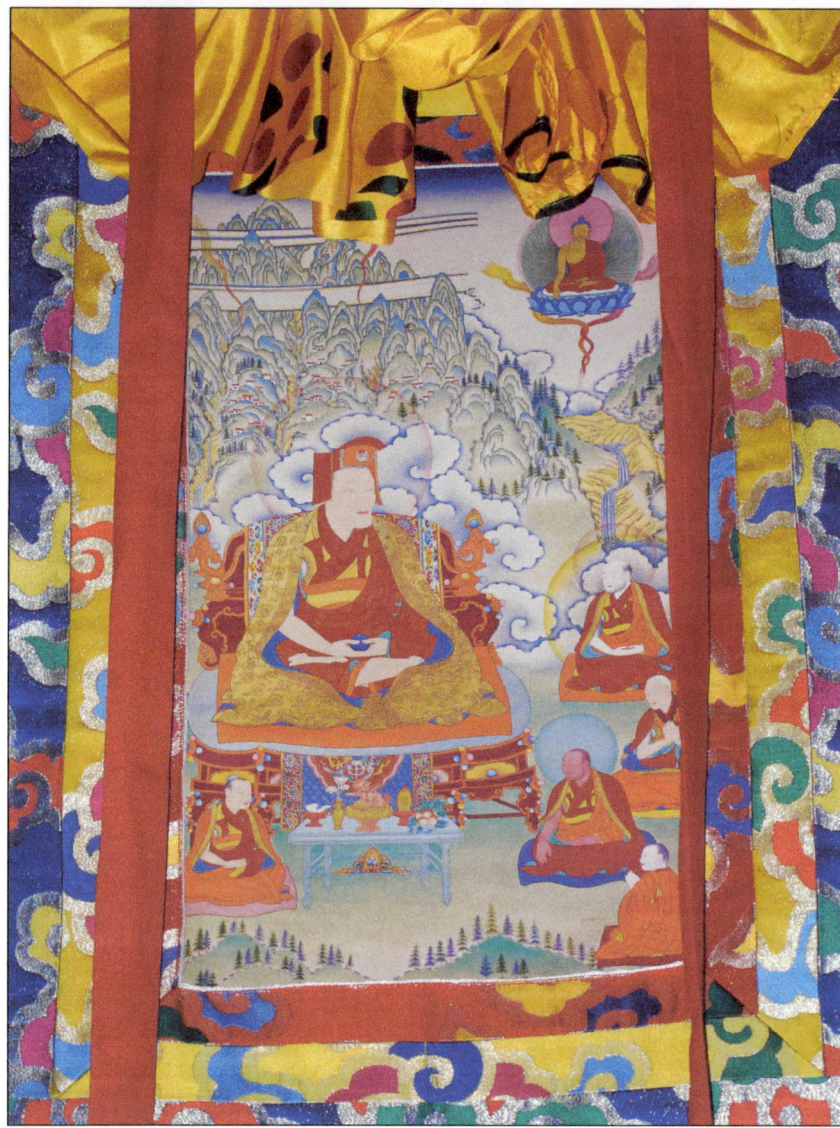

Gampopa
1251–1296

Dusum Khyenpa
1110–1193
1st Karmapa

The Golden Rosary

Drogon Rechen
1148–1219

Pomdrakpa
1170–1249

88 Understanding the Tibetan Buddhist Temple

Karma Pakshi
1204–1283
2nd Karmapa

Orgyenpa Rinchen Pal
1230–1309

Ranjung Dorje
1284–1339
3rd Karmapa

Gyalwa Yungton Dorje Pal
1284–1365

Rolpe Dorje
1340–1383
4th Karmapa

Khacho Wangpo
1350–1405
2nd Shamarpa

Deshin Shekpa
1384–1415
5th Karmapa

Ratnabadra (Richen Zangpo)
15th century

Chokyi Gyaltsen
1377–1448
1st Kenting Tai Situpa

Thongwa Donden
1416–1453
6th Karmapa

Bengar Jampal Zangpo

1427–1489

Paljor Dondrup

1424–1486

1st Goshir Gyaltsap Rinpoche

94 Understanding the Tibetan Buddhist Temple

Chodrak Gyatso
1454–1506
7th Karmapa

Tashi Paljor
1498–1541
3rd Kenting Tai Situpa

The Golden Rosary

Mikyo Dorje
1507–1554
8th Karmapa

Konchog Yanlak
1526–1583
5th Shamarpa

Wangchuk Dorje
1556–1603
9th Karmapa

Mipam Chokyi Wangchuk
1584–1629
6th Shamarpa

The Golden Rosary

Choying Dorje
1604–1674
10th Karmapa

Yeshe Nyingpo
1631–1694
7th Shamarpa

Yeshe Dorje
1676–1702
11th Karmapa

Palchen Chokyi Dhondrup
1733–1741
9th Shamarpa

Changchub Dorje
1703–1732
12th Karmapa

Chokyi Jungney
1699–1774
8th Kenting Tai Situpa

100 Understanding the Tibetan Buddhist Temple

Dudul Dorje
1733–1797
13th Karmapa

Mipam Chodrup Gyatso
1742–1793
10th Shamarpa

Missing
Pema Nyinje Wangpo
1774–1853
9th Kenting Tai Situpa

The Golden Rosary

Thekchok Dorje
1798–1868
14th Karmapa

Lodro Thaye
1813–1899
1st Jamgon Kongtrul

Kakyab Dorje
1871–1922
15th Karmapa

Pema Wangchuk Gyalpo
1886–1952
11th Kenting Tai Situpa

The Golden Rosary

Palden Khyentse Oser
1904–1952
2nd Jamgon Kongtrul

Rangjung Rigpe Dorje
1924–1981
16th Karmapa

Part III

The Consecration of Dzambhala

ABOUT DZAMBHALA

DZAMBHALA, known as Jambhala or Zambhala in variant spellings, is the Dharma Protector associated with wealth. He is sometimes linked with Kubera, the Hindu god of wealth, or with various Chinese gods of wealth, including Hotei (sometimes called the Laughing Buddha), Caishen, and Zao Jun, the Chinese kitchen god.

In the Vajrayana tradition, Dzambhala appears in five manifestations: green, white, yellow, red, and black. Of these, Yellow Dzambhala is considered the most powerful. All but Red Dzambhala appear as solitary heroes, while Red Dzambhala appears with his dakini consort. In all his manifestations, in his left hand he holds a magical mongoose that spits forth wish-fulfilling jewels, while in his right hand he holds a variety of objects depending on the manifestation.

According to HH Gyaltsen Sogdzin Rinpoche, "Because in this world, there are all kinds of wrathful and negative emotions or bad spirits, and sometimes they will harm you and other sentient beings, Dzambhala must take on such a wrathful and powerful form to protect us from these harmful spirits and negative karma. Especially, Dzambhala helps us minimize or decrease all misfortunes and obstacles and helps us increase all good fortune and happiness."

Also associated with Dzambhala are dadar blessing arrows and treasure vases. Treasure vases are sometimes buried under one's house. White Dzambhala is particularly associated with the discovery of Dharma treasures (*termas*) hidden by past masters for discovery in a later age. Prayers to him increase one's opportunity to reveal such treasures for the benefit of others.

I was fortunate to have the opportunity to witness the process of consecrating a shipment of new statues for the temple, including Dzambhala and a number of smaller auxiliary statues. This section of the book explains that process.

Unconsecrated statues
Ushnishavijaya, the Lady "Victorious Crown Ornament," *left*
Amitayus, the Buddha of Infinite Life, *right*

Ushnishavijaya is one of the three Long Life deities, along with Amitayus and White Tara. She is white, has three faces, and eight arms. Her first right hand holds a crossed vajra, second Amitabha on a white lotus, third an arrow, and fourth is in the supreme generosity mudra. The first left holds a vajra lasso, second a bow, third in the mudra of bestowing protection, and fourth in the meditative equipoise mudra holding a Long Life vase. Like all meditation deities, she is adorned with jewels and heavenly garments. Note too the white blessing cord hanging from her crown.

Unconsecrated statues are shipped with the bottoms open and the faces protected with cloth. The statues are filled with blessing materials and then sealed with a copper plate inscribed with a crossed vajra. There is a particular ceremony performed when the cloth is removed, called "Opening the Buddha's Eyes."

Unconsecrated statues

Red Dzambhala with consort

In this picture you can also see a small Garuda (winged protector) on the right, holding a varja, a dadar arrow, and other ritual implements. The thangka print in the background shows the Twenty-One Taras. Behind are undedicated memorial plaques.

Unconsecrated statues
Red Dzambhala with consort

A closer look. The upside down red base is for Palden Lhamo's mule.

Unconsecrated Statues | 111

Palden Lhamo
Prior to installation on the base

Dorje Legpa's goat
You can see both mounts in this shot, and the pegs used to attach each to its base.

Unconsecrated Statues 113

Three Porcelain Buddhas in the Chinese style
Each is about twenty-four inches high. They were not part of the consecration, but worth including here.

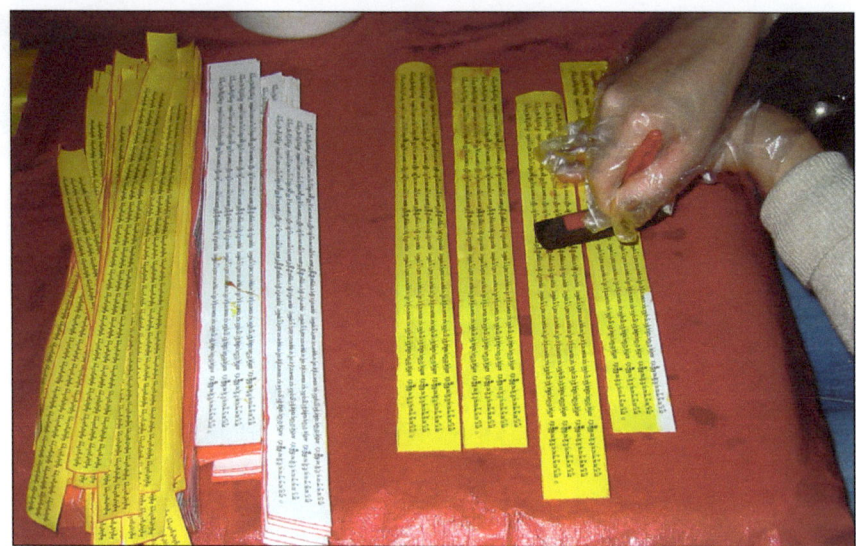

Consecration Mantras
Stages 1-3 in preparation

First, mantras are printed in quantity.
Secondly, the edges are painted red.
Next, the mantras are stained yellow with saffron water.

Consecration Mantras
Stages 4-5 in preparation

The sheets are left out to dry.
Then they are rolled up tightly.

 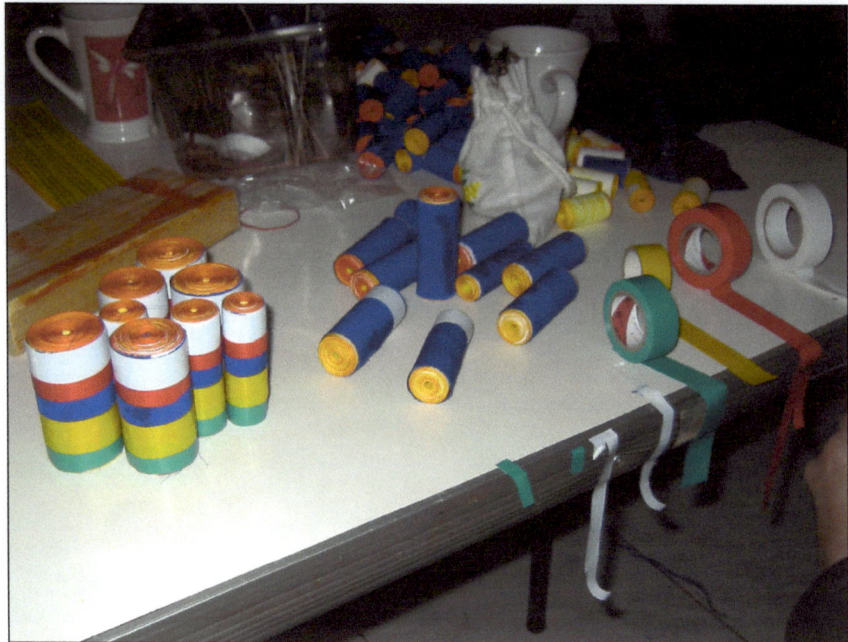

Consecration Mantras
Stages 6-7 in preparation

Once the mantras are dry and rolled, they are bound in cloth.
The five-coloured tape and cloth used to hold them equates to the five colours of the Buddhist flag, and the five Buddha families.

Consecration Mantras

Stage 8 in preparation

The completed mantras are ready for insertion inside statues.

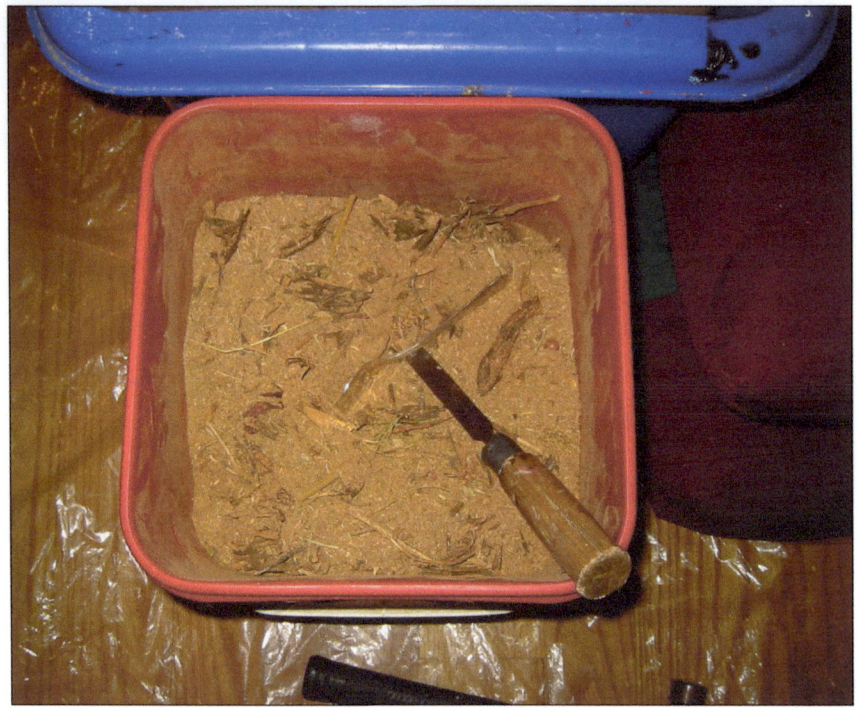

Consecration Ingredients
Mantras, ground incense, precious stones, coins

Above
Rolled mantras

Right
Ground incense

Opposite page >
Precious stones

The incense powder keeps everything tight and prevents it from rattling around inside the statues.

The precious stones in this case comprise crystals and beads from rosaries. In the case of specially-commissioned reliquary statues, other items such as sariras (artifacts from the cremation of revered teachers), body relics such as hair or teeth, cloth from a teacher's robes, or other items may be included.

Filling the base
First mantras

Lama Tashi Dondup placing items inside a statue. Facemasks are often used in Vajrayana offering rituals, in order to maintain the sanctity of the offered materials. Alternatively, you may see someone with a corner of their robe held over their mouth for the same purpose.

120 Understanding the Tibetan Buddhist Temple

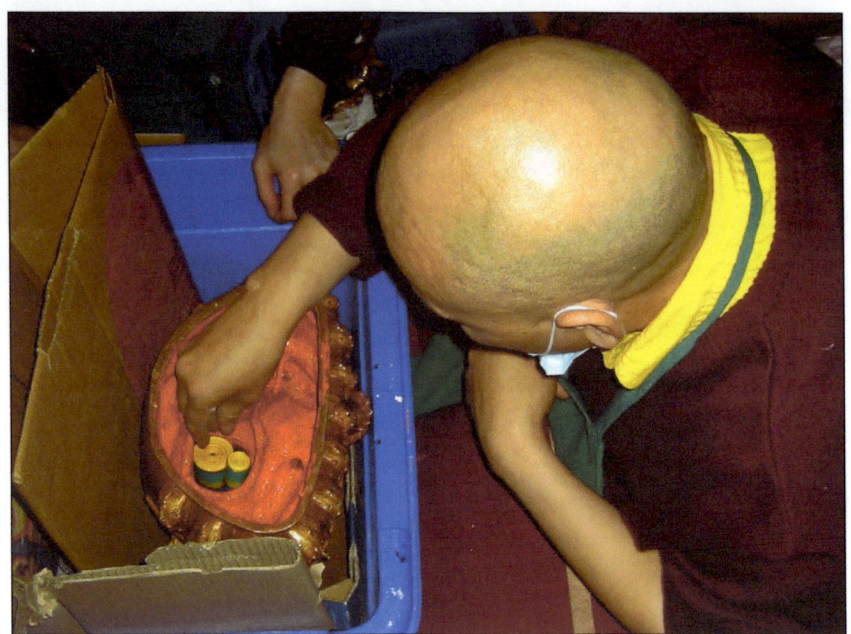

Filling the base
Beginning and finishing the process

Overleaf on the following two pages
Yellow and Red Dzambhalas
Closer views

Opposite page >
Dzambhala
Yellow Dzambhala, above
Red Dzambhala with Consort, below (two statues)

There are five manifestations of Dzambhala. This one is Yellow Dzambhala (considered the most powerful). His right leg is partially extended, resting on a lotus with a snail on it. He has two eyes and blue facial hair. His mouth is closed. His left hand holds a mongoose spitting out wish-fulfilling jewels. His right hand is holding a "mani" citron fruit. The statue is about thirty inches high.

    Below are smaller statues of Red Dzambhala, who is shown in union with his dakini consort. Red Dzambhala has a third wisdom-eye on his forehead and brown eyebrows that look like they are on fire. His right leg is partially extended, resting on a lotus with a conch shell on it. His consort holds a skull cup of nectar in her upraised left hand and a flaming wish-granting jewel in her upraised right hand.

122 Understanding the Tibetan Buddhist Temple

Yellow and Red Dzambhalas

DEDICATIONS

Refuge

With the wish to free all sentient beings,
I take refuge at all times
in the Buddha, Dharma and Sangha
until the attainment of full Enlightenment.

Today, in the presence of the Enlightened Ones,
inspired by compassion, wisdom, and joyous effort,
I generate the mind aspiring for full Buddhahood
for the sake of all living beings.

For as long as space endures
and for as long as sentient beings remain,
until then may I too abide
to dispel the misery of the world.

Short Mandala Offering

O, the ground with scent is blessed and with flowers strewn,
adorned with Mount Meru, the four lands, the sun and moon,
transformed as a Pure Land and then offered.
May all wandering beings enjoy this Buddha Realm.

Dedication of Merit

By whatever virtues we have done
and shall do from now until our Enlightenment,
may your body of form thus remain
within this land like a vajra immutable.
We entreat you, by your kindness, may all be auspicious,
Holy Venerable Ones.

A Long Life Prayer for the 17th Karmapa, Ogyen Trinley Dorje
Composed by the 12th Gyaltsab Rinpoche

Unborn, eternal, self-arising
Dharma nature
Arises as the miraculous
bodies of form;
May the three secrets of the Karmapa,
[body, speech, and mind]
be stable in the vajra nature
and may his limitless
Buddha-activity
spontaneously blaze.

Dear reader: Please forgive any errors or omissions; they are the fault of the author's misunderstanding.
You are encouraged to pursue further research into any topic that you find of interest, or that you think may be incorrect.
John Harvey Negru

www.ingramcontent.com/pod-product-compliance
Lightning Source LLC
Chambersburg PA
CBHW040537240426

43665CB00040B/70